First published 2016 by Retro Inc Books
www.retroinc.co.uk
© 2016

ISBN 978-09563290-97

Ella Cotton

Wankpuffin

A wonderful amalgamation of two words.
Wank is a British word for masturbation.
Puffin, taken from puffery, is a term for
exaggeration and hot air.
Donald Trump has been frequently called a
Wankpuffin.

SpunkOwl

The authors invention, as far as she is aware.

A general insult that conjures up images of a noctur-
nal prostitute or night-time cruiser.

Wanker

A British term for a habitual masturbator.

A silly idiot. Can be used as a term of endearment between mates.

Gasfanny

A woman who emits fanny farts after sexual
intercourse.
Also has origins in the 1944 film 'Fanny by Gaslight'.

Fanny gas is probably not flammable.

Junkie

A drug addict.
Derived from the slang term for heroin 'Junk'.

William S. Burroughs wrote the pulp novel about his
heroin addiction 'Junkie' in 1953.

Alternative spelling Junky

Shithead

Slang for a contemptible person without any brains.

An idiot.

Steve Martin called his dog Shithead in the film
'The Jerk'.

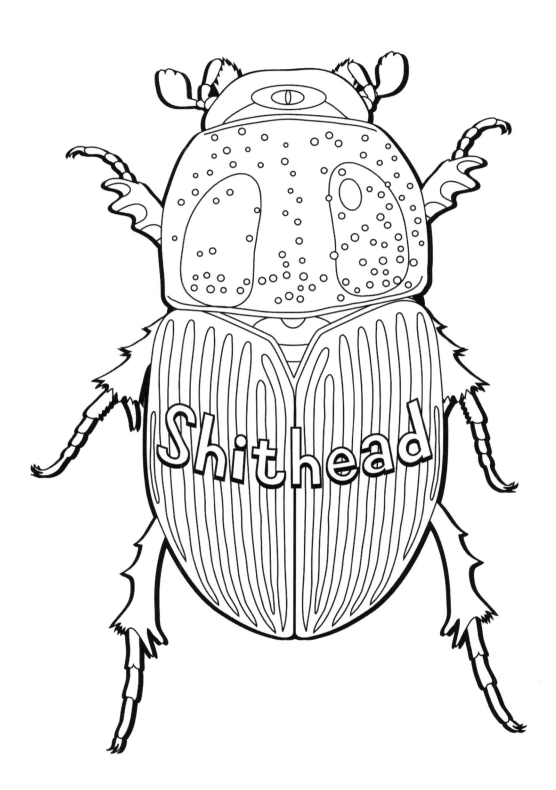

Monkey Tits

A stupid person.

Douchebag

An obnoxious person, typically male.

It's origins come from the rubber bag and tubing sold for vaginal irrigation.

Often used as a dodgy birth control measure or backdoor enema.

Cat Flap

A bisexual who 'swings both ways'

or a term for a vagina and labia.

Prat

Someone who has been an idiot but possibly
intentionally.
Prat refers to a backside.

The term pratfall meaning to fall on ones arse.
All clowns are therefore prats.
Which they are.

Knob Juggler

An insult to infer a person is a homosexual
or a habitual masturbator.

KNOB JUGGLER

Cockwomble

A male idiot or fool.

Bullshitter

A habitual liar who talks a lot of 'crap'.

A fantasist.

Bullshitter

Muppet

A term for a floppy idiot or silly fool.

Refers to the Muppet puppets created by
Jim Henson.

Tosspot

An idiot or Wanker.

Has its origins in referring to a drunkard.
Beer was originally served in public houses in
ceramic mugs.
Hence a drunk was always tossing his pot.

Knob Goblin

A person that really, really enjoys giving fellatio.

Ratbag

A popular Australian term for a troublemaker
that probably has its origins from the
'rat bag' that a rat catcher would keep his
dead pests in.

Fame Whore

An individual who is willing to do anything, however humiliating or demeaning, to achieve fame.

Think 'celebrity' reality shows where C list 'personalities' eat kangaroo balls or sit in a box full of spiders - that's a Fame Whore.

Slapper

British term for a lady who enjoys mucho sex,
with pretty much anyone.

Bumhead

General term of abuse.

However according to census records a
Fanny Bumhead lived in Bedfordshire, England
in 1861.

It is unsurprisingly a very rare surname in the UK.

Plonker

Light hearted insult for a dimwit.

Apparently has its origins from getting intoxicated on cheap 'plonk'.

Popularised by the series 'Only Fools and Horses'.

Toerag

A derogatory insult for a dirty or
worthless person.
Often applied to thieves.

Has its origins in a piece of dirty cloth wrapped
around a tramps foot in the place of a sock.

All wasps are toerags.

Toerag

Shyster

An unscrupulous, fraudulent, or deceptive person.

Probably derived from the German word 'Scheisse'
which translates as shit.

Bellend

The head, glans, of the male penis.

A foolish person or idiot.

Bellend

Thank You
for buying this book.
We hope you enjoyed it.
Please let us know what
you thought.

retroinc.co.uk

Thank you for purchasing this book.
We hope you enjoy it.

Please contact us with any comments you may have.
It's great to hear from readers.
Twitter @retrobooks

We are running a competition to find readers favourite
insults or swearwords.
The winner gets to see theirs designed by Ella and will receive a
signed print of it and other goodies.
Find out more via our website or facebook page:
facebook.com/retroincbooks

Twitter @retrobooks

19385507R00035

Printed in Great Britain
by Amazon